Romeo and Juliet

STUDY GUIDE

✳

Emily Hutchinson

GLOBE FEARON
EDUCATIONAL PUBLISHER

A Division of Simon & Schuster
Upper Saddle River, New Jersey

The Pacemaker Classics Study Guides

Plays

Antigone
Cyrano de Bergerac
A Doll's House
Hamlet
Julius Caesar
Macbeth
A Midsummer Night's Dream
Romeo and Juliet

Other Titles

The Adventures of Huckleberry Finn
The Adventures of Tom Sawyer
All Quiet on the Western Front
Anne Frank: The Diary of a Young Girl
The Call of the Wild
A Christmas Carol
The Count of Monte Cristo
Crime and Punishment
David Copperfield

The Deerslayer
Dracula
Dr. Jekyll and Mr. Hyde
Ethan Frome
Frankenstein
The Good Earth
The Grapes of Wrath
Great Expectations
Gulliver's Travels
Heart of Darkness
The Hound of the Baskervilles
The House of the Seven Gables
The Hunchback of Notre Dame
Jane Eyre
The Jungle
The Jungle Book
The Last of the Mohicans
The Mayor of Casterbridge
Moby Dick
The Moonstone

Oliver Twist
Narrative of the Life of Frederick
    Douglass, an American Slave
O Pioneers!
The Phantom of the Opera
The Prince and the Pauper
The Red Badge of Courage
Robinson Crusoe
The Scarlet Letter
The Sea-Wolf
A Tale of Two Cities
Tales of Edgar Allan Poe
The Three Musketeers
The Time Machine
Treasure Island
The Turn of the Screw
20,000 Leagues Under the Sea
Two Years Before the Mast
The War of the Worlds
Wuthering Heights

Executive Editor: Joan Carrafiello
Project Editor: Karen Bernhaut
Editorial Assistant: Keisha Carter
Marketing Manager: Marge Curson
Art Director: Joan Jacobus
Production Manager: Alan Dalgleish
Electronic Page Design: Maria Falkenberg
Cover Illustration: Karen Loccisano
Hand-marbled Paper: 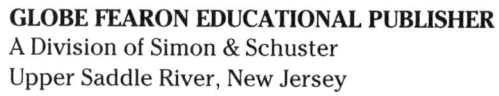 MOTH MARBLERS

ISBN 0-835-91219-1

Printed in the United States of America

4 5 6 7 8 9 10 03 02 01 00

 **GLOBE FEARON EDUCATIONAL PUBLISHER**
A Division of Simon & Schuster
Upper Saddle River, New Jersey

Contents

To the Teacher

The Content

The Pacemaker Classics Study Guides are a series of literature-based study units for secondary and adult students. Each study guide is designed to extend and enrich one of the Pacemaker Classics, though it may also be used with the original version of the work. Each study guide includes teacher's notes and 35 reproducible student project sheets. Of these, 28 are based on units, or sections from the text, with 7 project sheets corresponding to each unit.

The pattern for these 7 project sheets is as follows: Unit 1: Setting the Scene, Prereading, Key Words, Point of View, Language Lab, Wild Card, and Challenge; Units 2–4: Prereading, Character Study, Key Words, Point of View, Language Lab, Wild Card, and Challenge. The Wild Card might be based on cause and effect, problems and solutions, analyzing plot, sequencing, extending the story, or any other skill that is suggested by the unit. The challenge activities are on a more difficult level than the other project sheets and are not necessarily recommended for all students.

A 2-page final exam follows the unit project sheets. The last 5 pages are open-ended project sheets, including activities for working with the glossary, sequencing the story, understanding the times, and writing a book report. These project sheets should be used after the students have completed the play.

Students should be provided with a copy of Teacher's Notes, page v (About the Playwright/About the Times/About Elizabethan Theater). The information on this page is necessary for them to complete some of the open-ended project sheets.

The Methodology

A whole-language approach is implicit in the instructional design of this series. The reproducible exercise pages encourage students to use many forms of communication and draw on their prior knowledge to increase their enjoyment of the play, as well as their comprehension and thinking abilities. For example, a vocabulary-based project might include reading for context clues, as well as doing some creative writing using key vocabulary words. Thinking, reading, discussing, listening, and writing are only a few of the skills students will be practicing. This whole-language approach is designed to help students personalize and integrate what they are learning into their own lives.

This icon  indicates any activities that are especially suited for cooperative group work. However, you may wish to organize cooperative learning groups or assign partners to work together for most or all of the activities.

Students will need to be familiar with terms like **character, plot, sequence, setting,** and **journal** as they do the worksheets. For this reason, a glossary of terms used in this book is included. You should duplicate this glossary and distribute a copy to each student.

Teacher's Notes

About the Playwright

Although Shakespeare is regarded as the finest poet and playwright of the Renaissance, very little is known about his life. We know that he was baptized in 1564 in Stratford-on-Avon, so we assume he was born in that year. We also know that he married Anne Hathaway when he was 18 and she was 26. Within three years they had three children.

There is evidence that Shakespeare moved to London sometime between 1585 and 1588, leaving his family in Stratford. He apparently lived in London for the next 25 years or so. He started his career as an actor, and he began to write plays shortly after. From 1592 to 1594, the London theaters were closed because of the plague. There is no record of what Shakespeare did during this time. We can assume he was writing plays. By 1597, he had written at least 12 plays, including *Romeo and Juliet*.

In 1599, a group of the leading actors of London got together to build and run a new playhouse. Shakespeare was one of them. The theater, called the Globe, became one of the most famous theaters of the day. Because of its success, Shakespeare became a fairly wealthy man.

He bought a fine house in Stratford in 1597, and his wife and daughters moved into it sometime later. He joined them there, probably in 1612. He died in the house in 1616, leaving Anne his "second best bed" in his will.

About the Times

Shakespeare's most productive years were during what is called the Elizabethan Age in England. This period is also known as the English Renaissance. During the reign (1558–1603) of Elizabeth I, drama emerged as the most important literary genre. London's first public theater, built in 1576 by James Burbage, was so popular that by 1585, a second playhouse was being used.

Elizabethan London, a bustling medieval city, was the center of England's social, business, and intellectual life. It was the only city in England that was fully under the influence of the Renaissance, that flowering of art and culture in Italy, France, and Spain. Most of the printers and publishers of England were in London. Theaters for the public performance of drama in England were found only in London, as well.

About Elizabethan Theater

Theaters in Shakespeare's time were designed very differently from modern theaters. The stage jutted out into the audience, taking up the space now used by the first few rows of seats. This stage had no curtain to be raised, lowered, or opened, and stage props were minimal. Sets were not nearly as elaborate as they are in the modern theater. In fact, the audience had to use its imagination to believe that the same set could work for both a street scene and a ballroom scene.

The rear of the stage had a small curtained area, which was often used as an inner room, a tomb, or a prison. Balconies on the sides of the stage were used for upper decks of ships, balconies of houses, and prison windows. Because there was no curtain, playwrights had to devise ways to get "dead bodies" off the stage. They had to be carried away as part of the action of the play. In the modern theater, on the other hand, the curtain is closed and the stage is cleared for the next scene. When theaters were not available, plays were performed in public places, such as inns and taverns.

In addition to these physical discrepancies, there is also another important difference between Elizabethan and contemporary theater. In Elizabethan times, women were not allowed to act. Therefore, most women's roles were played by boys who were often recruited from the boys' church choirs in London.

Teacher's Notes   (continued)

Synopsis

The Capulets and the Montagues, two prominent families of Verona, Italy, have been feuding for years. Servants of the rival houses meet and quarrel. Their superiors, Benvolio and Tybalt, join in. The heads of the families arrive and are prevented from joining the fight by Prince Escalus, who says that any more fighting will be punishable by death.

Romeo Montague has been brooding over his unrequited love for Rosaline. His cousin, Benvolio, tells him to forget Rosaline and look at other beauties. Just then, an illiterate Capulet servant asks for their help in reading a guest list. In this way, Romeo and Benvolio learn that a masked ball is being given that night at the Capulet house, and Rosaline is invited. Benvolio sees this as an opportunity for Romeo to compare Rosaline to other girls.

Before the party, Lord Capulet talks to Paris, who wants to marry Juliet. Capulet is reluctant because Juliet is his only child and is not yet 14. Even so, he asks Paris to attend the party and to approach Juliet. If Juliet is agreeable to the idea of marriage, Capulet will also agree.

At the party, Romeo meets Juliet. They fall in love at first sight. Later, they find out that they belong to the rival families. After the party, Romeo climbs the wall into the Capulet orchard. Juliet comes out on her balcony. They declare their love and make plans to marry. Romeo visits Friar Laurence to arrange for the wedding. The Friar hopes that the marriage will bring peace between the two families.

After the secret marriage, Tybalt, a Capulet who had recognized Romeo at the party, insults Romeo on the street. Romeo's friend Mercutio fights Tybalt in a duel. Romeo, now related to Tybalt, tries to stop the fight, but Tybalt kills Mercutio. Romeo then fights Tybalt and kills him. Prince Escalus banishes Romeo from Verona.

Romeo and Juliet spend one night together before he leaves. He hopes to be pardoned so that he can return. Juliet is grief-stricken. Her father, thinking she is grieving for her cousin Tybalt, arranges for her marriage to Paris. He thinks the marriage will cheer her up. When she objects, her parents become angry and tell her that she must obey them and marry Paris. Even Juliet's nurse tells her that Paris is a better match than the banished Romeo. Juliet turns to Friar Laurence for help.

Friar Laurence tells Juliet his plan for her to get out of the wedding. He gives her a potion that will make her appear dead for 42 hours. She will be put in the family tomb, and the Friar and Romeo will be there when she wakes up. Then she can leave Verona with Romeo. That night, Juliet drinks the potion and falls into a deep sleep. The Nurse finds her the next morning, and everyone thinks she is dead. The joyful wedding plans must be changed into funeral plans.

Romeo's servant brings him word that Juliet is dead. The Friar's message—that she is not really dead—fails to reach Romeo. Romeo decides to join Juliet in death and buys some poison before setting out for Verona. Romeo finds Paris at the Capulet tomb and kills him when he will not leave. Romeo then kisses Juliet, drinks the poison, and dies. The Friar arrives just as Juliet is waking up. He tries to get her to leave the tomb, but she won't go. The Friar leaves, and Juliet then kills herself with Romeo's dagger. When the families discover the tragic truth, they agree to end their fighting.

For convenience, each play has been divided into four study units. This chart shows how the study units in the Pacemaker version of *Romeo and Juliet* correspond to the divisions of the original text.

Study Unit	Pacemaker Classic Acts	Original Text Acts
1	1	1
2	2	2
3	3	3
4	4–5	4–5

About the Characters

Romeo (ROH-mee-oh) is a young man of Verona.

Lord Montague (MAHN-tuh-gyoo) is Romeo's father.

Lady Montague is Romeo's mother.

Mercutio (mer-KYOO-shee-oh) is Romeo's friend.

Benvolio (behn-VOH-lee-oh) is Romeo's cousin.

Balthasar (BAL-thuh-zahr) is Romeo's servant.

Abram is Lord Montague's servant.

Friar Laurence (FRY-er LAW-rihns) is a Franciscan priest.

Friar John is a friend of Friar Laurence.

Juliet (JOO-lee-eht) is a young girl of Verona.

Lord Capulet (CAP-yoo-leht) is Juliet's father.

Lady Capulet is Juliet's mother.

The Nurse is Juliet's nurse since infancy.

Sampson and **Gregory** are servants of Lord Capulet.

Tybalt (TIHB-uhlt) is Juliet's cousin.

Paris is a cousin of Prince Escalus.

Prince Escalus (ES-cuh-lihs) is the ruler of Verona.

Audio-Visual Suggestions

- There are several movie versions of *Romeo and Juliet*, the best of which is directed by Franco Zeffirelli and stars Leonard Whiting and Olivia Hussey. This 1968 version features a beautiful music score, exquisite cinematography, and Oscar-winning costumes. A 1936 version directed by George Cukor and starring Norma Shearer and Leslie Howard, a 1954 version directed by Renato Castellani and starring Laurence Harvey and Susan Shentall, and a 1966 ballet version directed by Paul Czinner and starring Margot Fonteyn and Rudolf Nureyev, are also available.
- You might wish to show the students the film *West Side Story*, which was based on the *Romeo and Juliet* story. Discuss similarities and differences.
- Obtain and display pictures of William Shakespeare, the Globe Theatre, 16th-century clothing and architecture, and various artistic representations of some scenes from the play.
- Play the Pacemaker Classic audiotape of *Romeo and Juliet*. Have students follow along as they listen to this word-for-word reading of the Pacemaker version.
- On a map, point out the location of Verona in Northern Italy.

Notes on Unit 1

Unit 1 corresponds to Act 1 of the play. Scene 1 opens in Verona, a city in Northern Italy. The Capulets and the Montagues, two prominent families, have been fighting for years. One day, a fight breaks out in the street between the servants and members of the families. Prince Escalus, the ruler of Verona, declares that any more fighting will be considered civil disobedience and punishable by death.

Romeo Montague's parents are worried about him, and they ask their nephew Benvolio to find out why Romeo has been so depressed. Benvolio discovers that Romeo has been brooding over his love for Rosaline, who does not return his affection.

In Scene 2, Count Paris asks Lord Capulet for Juliet's hand in marriage. Capulet says he will approve if Juliet agrees. He invites Paris to a masked ball that evening, and he sends a servant out to invite the people on his guest list.

The servant, who cannot read, approaches Romeo and Benvolio on the street and asks them to read the list for him. Rosaline's name is on the list. Benvolio sees this as an opportunity for Romeo to compare Rosaline to other girls. Going to the party as uninvited guests is, of course, dangerous for them, but the two young men are daring enough to welcome the challenge.

In Scene 3, Lady Capulet and Juliet's nurse talk to her about Paris and about the possibility of marriage. Juliet says she is not interested in marriage, but she agrees to be gracious to Paris that night.

In Scene 4, Romeo and his associates make their way to the party. Romeo has a feeling of impending doom.

In Scene 5, Romeo meets Juliet at the party. They fall in love at first sight. Later, they find out that they belong to the rival families.

Unit 1 Project Sheets Answer Key:

Exercise 1: For 1 and 2, answers to the first parts are given. Answers to the second parts will vary. 1. whether she will ever fall in love, her health, her relationships with her friends; 2. ride a horse, read, defend himself with a sword; 3. Answers will vary.

Exercise 2: Answers will vary.

Exercise 3: A—Wording of answers will vary but should approximate the following: 1. to break in upon with noise or some distraction; 2. promise; 3. yes; 4. tell that person your opinion about the best course of action; 5. a heavy load; 6. not busy; 7. destiny; 8. a scoundrel, cad, or rascal; 9. Answers will vary.
B—Answers will vary.

Exercise 4: Answers will vary.

Exercise 5: Answers will vary.

Exercise 6: Answers will vary. Possible responses are given. 1. He draws his sword. 2. She snaps her fingers, as if to say something had slipped her mind. 3. He holds out his hand. He takes a mask from his friend. 4. He points toward the kitchen. 5. He nods, not wishing to point, and looks in Juliet's direction.

Exercise 7: Answers will vary.

Notes on Unit 2

Unit 2 corresponds to Act 2 of the play. In Scene 1, which is right after the party, Romeo climbs the wall into the Capulet orchard. Benvolio and Mercutio look for him, but they cannot find him. Romeo does not respond to their calls.

In Scene 2, Juliet comes out on her balcony, and Romeo hears her talking about him. He speaks to her, and they declare their love and make plans to marry. Juliet plans to send a messenger the next morning to find out where and when she and Romeo will be wed.

In Scene 3, Romeo visits Friar Laurence to make arrangements for the wedding. The Friar agrees, hoping that the marriage will bring peace between the two families.

In Scene 4, Romeo sends word through the Nurse to Juliet to meet him at Friar Laurence's cell in the afternoon for the wedding.

In Scene 5, Juliet waits for the Nurse to return and tell her the plans. When the Nurse arrives, she talks more about her own pains than about Romeo. Finally, Juliet gets the Nurse to tell her what Romeo said.

In Scene 6, Romeo and Juliet meet at Friar Laurence's cell for the wedding ceremony.

Unit 2 Project Sheets Answer Key:

Exercise 1: A—Answers to the first parts are given. Answers to the second parts will vary. 1. Romeo and Juliet are declaring their love for each other. 2. Romeo and Juliet will soon be married by the Friar.
B—Answers will vary.

Exercise 2: Answers to the first parts are given. Answers to the second parts will vary. 1. has never been in love; 2. if Romeo's name were Tim, he would still be wonderful; 4. does not like Paris.

Exercise 3: A—Answers to the first parts are given. Answers to the second parts will vary.
1. mix up; 2. reject; 3. many kinds; 4. enthusiastic.
B—Answers will vary.

Exercise 4: Answers will vary.

Exercise 5: Answers to the first parts are given. Answers to the second parts will vary. 1. metaphor (given); 2. simile; 3. metaphor; 4. simile; 5. simile; 6. simile.

Exercise 6: Answers to the first parts are given. Answers to the second parts will vary. 1. Romeo Hides; 2. Romeo and Juliet Declare Their Love; 3. The Friar Agrees to the Marriage; 4. Romeo Tells the Nurse the Plan; 5. The Nurse Tells Juliet the Plan; 6. Romeo and Juliet Meet for Their Wedding.

Exercise 7: Answers will vary.

Notes on Unit 3

Unit 3 corresponds to Act 3 of the play. Benvolio and Mercutio meet at the public square. Tybalt, a Capulet who had recognized Romeo at the party, approaches them, looking for Romeo. When Romeo appears, Tybalt insults him, hoping to goad him into a duel. But Romeo, now secretly related to Tybalt through marriage, tries to avoid a scuffle. Mercutio is angered by this and takes up Romeo's defense. He is killed in the ensuing duel, partly because of Romeo's intervention. Romeo then avenges Mercutio by killing Tybalt. Benvolio rushes Romeo away from the scene and explains the events to Prince Escalus. Because of the circumstances, the Prince defers the death sentence. Instead, Romeo is banished forever from Verona.

In Scene 2, the Nurse tells Juliet what has happened. Torn by her grief for Tybalt and her love for Romeo, Juliet justifies Romeo's behavior with the thought that Tybalt would have killed Romeo if he had had the chance. The Nurse promises to arrange for Romeo to spend one night with Juliet before he has to leave.

In Scene 3, Friar Laurence tries to comfort Romeo, who is hiding from the authorities in the Friar's cell. He tells Romeo that he will not be put to death but must leave Verona instead. Romeo thinks that separation from Juliet will be worse than death. The Nurse arrives and assures Romeo of Juliet's wish to see him that night. The Friar urges Romeo to spend the night with his bride before leaving for Mantua. The Friar tells Romeo that he will keep Romeo informed of any news that might lead to his pardon.

In Scene 4, Lord Capulet and Paris again discuss the possibility of Paris's marriage to Juliet. Capulet impulsively agrees to hold the wedding in three days, hoping to end her grief. He thinks she is crying because of Tybalt's death.

In Scene 5, Romeo and Juliet say good-bye at dawn. Then Lady Capulet comes to Juliet's room and tells her about the wedding plans. Juliet is horrified to find out that her parents want her to marry Paris, and she refuses. Her parents angrily tell her she must go through with the wedding. Even the Nurse tells her that Paris is a better catch than the banished Romeo. Juliet decides to turn to the Friar for help.

Unit 3 Project Sheets Answer Key:

Exercise 1: A—Answers will vary.
B—Answers will vary.
Exercise 2: A—1. Mercutio; 2. Tybalt; 3. Friar Laurence; 4. Romeo; 5. the Nurse; 6. Prince Escalus; 7. Lady Capulet; 8. Benvolio; 9. Juliet; 10. Capulet.
B—Answers will vary.
Exercise 3: A—1. insult, excuse, slash, quarrel; 2. comfort; farewell; weeping; jealous.
B—Answers will vary.
Exercise 4: Answers will vary.
Exercise 5: Answers will vary.
Exercise 6: Answers will vary.
Exercise 7: Answers will vary.

Notes on Unit 4

Unit 4 corresponds to Acts 4 and 5 of the play. In Act 4, Scene 1, Paris is talking with Friar Laurence about his upcoming marriage to Juliet when Juliet arrives at the Friar's cell. After Paris leaves, Juliet expresses her grief, and Friar Laurence comes up with a plan. He gives her a small bottle of liquid to drink the night before the wedding. When she drinks it, she will appear dead for 42 hours. She will be put into the family tomb. Meanwhile, the Friar will send word to Romeo to come to Verona, be there when she wakes up, and take her back to Mantua with him.

In Act 4, Scene 2, Juliet pretends to go along with the wedding plans.

In Act 4, Scene 3, Juliet drinks the potion and falls on her bed, unconscious.

In Act 4, Scene 4, the wedding morning has arrived. The Nurse goes to wake Juliet.

In Act 4, Scene 5, the Nurse finds Juliet, apparently dead. The joyous wedding preparations must be stopped, and the funeral arrangements must be made.

In Act 5, Scene 1, Balthasar, Romeo's servant, travels to Mantua and tells Romeo that Juliet is dead. Romeo buys a powerful poison from a druggist and sets out for Verona, planning to join Juliet in death.

In Act 5, Scene 2, Friar Laurence sends Friar John to Mantua with a letter for Romeo. The letter explains the plan. Two days later, Friar John returns to tell Friar Laurence that he was unable to deliver the letter because of a quarantine in the city. Friar Laurence, realizing that his plan has been ruined, hurries to the Capulet tomb to be there when Juliet awakens.

In Act 5, Scene 3, Romeo arrives at the Capulet tomb and finds Paris there. They fight, and Paris is killed. Romeo enters the tomb, sees Juliet, and drinks the poison. He dies immediately. Friar Laurence arrives as Juliet awakens. When she sees Romeo dead, she refuses to leave. Frightened by the sounds of guards, Friar Laurence flees. Juliet then kills herself, using Romeo's dagger. The watchmen alert the city about what has happened, and the families assemble at the tomb. Prince Escalus and both families listen to Friar Laurence's account of what has happened. Montague and Capulet join hands and put their feud to rest.

Unit 4 Project Sheets Answer Key:

Exercise 1: Answers will vary.

Exercise 2: Answers will vary.

Exercise 3: Answers to the first parts are given. Answers to the second parts will vary. 1. very well, all right; 2. remainder, what is left; 3. being in a flat, horizontal position; 4. a small room, as for a prisoner or a monk; 5. a small amount of liquid in a somewhat round shape.

Exercise 4: Answers will vary.

Exercise 5: A—Answers to the first parts are given. Answers to the second parts will vary. 1. Paris has not had a chance to speak to Juliet about love. 2. Capulet is so upset he can't even talk. 3. Paris is saying he will cry for Juliet for a long time. 4. Romeo is saying he can't live without Juliet and will soon be dead. B—Answers will vary.

Exercise 6: Answers will vary.

Exercise 7: Answers will vary.

Final Exam Answer Key:

A—1. Montague and Capulet; 2. Verona, Italy; 3. He loved Rosaline, but she didn't love him; 4. Rosaline would be there; 5. Paris; 6. the same night they met; 7. He killed Tybalt in a duel; 8. the plan concerning Juliet; 9. He took poison; 10. she died of grief after Romeo was sent away. B—Answers will vary.

Glossary

advice   a suggestion about how to do something

Example: My advice to you is to work harder.

aside   a speech made by an actor that the other characters in the play presumably cannot hear. It reveals the character's inner thoughts to the audience.

Example: In an aside, the villain revealed his plan to kill the king.

brainstorm   to list ideas as fast as they come, without commenting on or organizing them in any way; usually done by a group of people working together

Example: The children brainstormed until they had a list of 50 ideas.

cause   anything that produces an effect, action, or result

Example: A virus was the cause of his illness.

character   a person in a story or play

Example: Romeo Montague is an important character in *Romeo and Juliet.*

chart   a graph or some other visual way of presenting information

chorus   in Elizabethan drama, a person who recites the prologue and/or the epilogue; in ancient Greek drama, the performers who explain and elaborate on the main action

Example: In *Romeo and Juliet* the chorus recites the prologue.

comparison   a way of showing how two things are alike or different

Example: The comparison showed that this red is much brighter than that one.

conflict   a battle or struggle; the opposition of two forces or ideas

Example: The conflict between the father and his son involved using the car without permission.

context clues   hints in a sentence or paragraph that help tell what an unknown word means

Example: Through context clues, Wesley figured out that *enormous* means the same thing as *huge.*

cooperative learning group   a small group of students who work together to share knowledge and help one another learn

Example: Alice learned better study habits from her cooperative learning group.

diagram   a type of chart; a way of showing something visually so it's easier to understand

Example: This diagram will show you how to put the chair together.

dialogue   the words that characters in a story say to each other

Example: The author has written some very funny dialogue in the second chapter.

diary   a written record of a person's experiences or thoughts

Example: Janette wrote in her diary every day.

dramatic irony   the difference between what a character thinks and what the reader or audience knows to be true

Example: The fact that the Nurse thinks Juliet is dead on her wedding day is an example of dramatic irony.

effect   a direct result

Example: The effect of lying in the sun for too long can be a bad sunburn.

epilogue   a short section at the end of a story that often takes place well after the main events

Glossary (continued)

Example: The epilogue described the lives of the characters ten years after they got married.

introduction the opening part of a story

Example: The introduction to the story explained how the writer thought of the idea for it.

journal a daily record of activities or thoughts; similar to a diary

Example: Tom kept a journal on his trip to Europe.

motive a reason for doing something

Example: His motive for working at two jobs was to earn extra money to buy a new car.

opinion something that a person believes is true

Example: Mick's opinion was that the area was dangerous.

passage a line or several lines from a story or book

Example: That passage from the novel was difficult to understand.

playwright writer of a play; dramatist

Example: The playwright of *Romeo and Juliet* is William Shakespeare.

plot the events that take place in a story

Example: The plot was very simple: man trains for race, man runs race, man wins race.

point of view the position or angle from which someone sees something

Example: The point of view was through the eyes of an outside observer.

prediction what someone says is going to happen

Example: Jo's prediction was that it would rain.

prologue part of the story that comes before the main action; an introduction

Example: In the prologue the author introduces the reader to the main character.

quotation the exact words that someone says

Example: Here is a quotation from the speech: "No new taxes!"

sequence the order in which something happens

Example: The sequence of events led to the capture of the criminal.

setting the place and time of a story or event

Example: The setting of the story was San Francisco during the Gold Rush days.

simile a comparison using the words *like* or *as*

Example: He ran like a rabbit.

soliloquy a long speech made by a character who is alone which reveals the character's private thoughts and feelings to the audience.

Example: Juliet's soliloquy before she takes the sleeping potion shows that she is afraid something might go wrong.

stage directions information given in a play about the costumes, lighting, scenery, setting, and the characters' movements and ways of speaking

Example: In Act 2, Scene 1, the following stage directions are given: Mercutio listens for an answer, but none comes.

symbol something that stands for something else

Example: The flag is a symbol of our country.

Setting the Scene

Name _____   Date _____

The **setting** of a play is the time and place in which it happens. The time for *Romeo and Juliet* is the late 16th century, probably the 1590s. The place is Verona, Italy. People lived much shorter lives than we do today. Juliet, at age 13, was somewhat young for marriage. Romeo, at about 16, was just about the right age. There were no modern conveniences like electricity, cars, trains, or telephones. Gentlemen learned the art of fencing, or sword fighting. Poor people did not learn to read. Women were very dependent on their fathers and their husbands. It was normal for parents to arrange a daughter's marriage.

Think about the setting of *Romeo and Juliet.* Imagine what life must have like then and there. Read the first two sentences below and check the item or items that you think make sense. Then write your reasons. Write an answer to the third question.

---

1. A wealthy young woman in Italy in 1590 might worry about _____.

    _____ whether she will fall in love   _____ what is on TV

    _____ what movie to see   _____ her health

    _____ her friendships   _____ if she can afford a computer

    The reason I think so is _____
    _____

2. A wealthy young man in the year 1595 would probably know how to _____.

    _____ drive a car   _____ ride a horse

    _____ read   _____ defend himself with a sword

    _____ play an electric guitar   _____ program a VCR

    The reason I think so is _____
    _____

3. If you could have chosen when to live, would you have chosen the 1590s or now? Why?

    _____

    _____

Prereading

Name _____ Date _____

A. Before you begin reading the play, look at the cover illustration and the illustrations in Act 1. Complete each sentence below.

---

1. The art on the book cover suggests that the story takes place in

_____

_____

Why do you think so? _____

2. The art in Act 1, Scene 2 shows that the characters

_____

_____

Why do you think so? _____

3. The art in Act 1, Scene 5 shows that

_____

_____

Why do you think so? _____

4. What do you think the characters might do after the scene shown in the art for Act 1, Scene 5?

_____

_____

B. Save your paper. After you read Act 1, look at your answer to question 4 above. What are the differences between your answer and what happens in the play? Write your answer on the lines below.

_____

_____

_____

_____

_____

Key Words

Name _____ Date _____

A. Read the sentences below. Make a good guess at what each word in bold type means. Write the meanings on the lines.

---

1. Prince Escalus was getting very tired of the fighting between the Capulets and the Montagues. He did not want them to **disturb** the peace again.

   Disturb means _____.

2. Rosaline had made a **vow** that she would never marry. This promise was the reason for Romeo's unhappiness.

   If you **vow** to do something, you _____.

3. Lord Capulet said he would **consent** to the marriage of Juliet and Paris only if Juliet liked the idea.

   If you **consent** to marry someone, your answer is _____.

4. Benvolio gave Romeo some **advice**. He said that Romeo had to try to forget Rosaline, for his own good.

   If you give **advice** to someone, you _____.

5. Romeo's love for Rosaline was a **burden**. Mercutio thought he should get rid of the heavy load.

   A **burden** is _____.

6. Mercutio said that dreams were the children of an **idle** brain. When he wasn't doing anything, he had more time for dreaming.

   Something that is **idle** is _____.

7. Romeo thought that **fate** directed his life. He believed that it was his destiny to go through certain things.

   Fate means about the same as _____.

8. Tybalt called Romeo a **villain**. Only a scoundrel, a cad, and a rascal would sneak into an enemy's party.

   Another word for **villain** is _____.

9. Lord Capulet told Tybalt not to be **rude** to Romeo, even if he belonged to the Montague family. After all, Romeo was a polite and fine young man.

   An example of being **rude** to someone would be _____.

B. In a dictionary, look up the meaning of each word in bold type. How close were your guesses?

Date _____

... talking to some of her friends. She is telling
... d the way he acts around her. On the lines
... aline might say.

_____

_____

_____

___

_____

_____

_____

_____

B. Imagine that Paris was watching Romeo and Juliet when they first met.
How do you think he felt? What might he say about it?

_____

_____

_____

_____

_____

_____

_____

Language Lab   **5**

Name _____   Date _____

The lines below come from the play. Read them and answer the questions
that follow. Use the back of this sheet if you need more room.

---

1. "Listen, you beasts who cool your rage / With blood that flows from your
   own veins." (page 4)

   Think about a situation that these words might be applied to today. Perhaps
   it is something you heard about on the news or saw in a movie. Describe
   the situation and tell what happened.

   _____

   _____

2. "At my humble house, you will see beauties / That, like stars, make
   nighttime bright." (page 8)

   Think about beauties you have seen that seem to make the nighttime bright.
   What qualities do they have?

   _____

   _____

3. "Look at his face as if it were a book." (page 12)

   Think about a face that you have tried to read like a book. What clues did
   that face give you about what the person might have been thinking?

   _____

   _____

4. "My soul is so heavy that / I am stuck to the ground." (page 13)

   Think about a time you or someone you know had a heavy soul. It might
   have been caused by love, work, or school. Describe the situation and what
   was done about it.

   _____

   _____

5. "You lied to me, sight. / For I never saw true beauty till this night." (page 20)

   Think about a time that you saw a very beautiful sight. Describe it and tell
   how you felt when you saw it.

   _____

   _____

Writing Stage Directions

Name _____ Date _____

In the original Shakespeare plays, there are very few stage directions. Some editions of Shakespeare have stage directions that were added later by other people. Read the following lines from the play. On the blank lines, write any stage directions that would make the performance easier for an actor. See the box below for ideas. You may use them, or you may write your own.

He draws his sword.
He points toward the kitchen.
He nods, not wishing to point,
   and looks in Juliet's direction.
He holds out his hand.
He points his sword, as if to
   threaten Benvolio.

He takes a mask from his friend.
She snaps her fingers, as if to say
   something had slipped her mind.
He grabs him by the shoulder to
   turn him around.

---

1. TYBALT: Benvolio, do you fight with servants?
   Turn, and face your death!

   _____

2. LADY CAPULET: Nurse, please leave us.
   No, wait a minute! I just remembered.
   You should hear this, too.

   _____

3. MERCUTIO: Now, give me a mask to wear.

   _____

   We're almost there.

   _____

4. FIRST SERVANT: Take the stools away.
   Move the sideboard.
   Take the silver platters to the kitchen.

   _____

5. ROMEO [*to a* SERVANT]: Who is that lady?
   Who gives richness to the hand of that knight
   By simply holding it?

   _____

Challenge

Name _____   Date _____

A. Act 1 opens with a Prologue. In this Prologue, the chorus tells the audience what will happen in the play. The chorus also hints that the characters were doomed from the beginning. Read the Prologue again and then answer the following questions.

---

1. Do you think the Prologue gives away too much of the story? Explain your answer. _____

_____

_____

_____

2. Why would you want to read a story or a play, if you already know the ending? Write three reasons. _____

_____

_____

_____

B. The Prologue tells the audience that "Their love is doomed by the family feud." From the start, Romeo and Juliet had the feeling that their love was doomed. Find some lines from the play that prove this. Write them below.

---

1. Act 1, Scene 4, Romeo: _____

_____

_____

_____

2. Act 1, Scene 5, Romeo: _____

_____

_____

_____

3. Act 1, Scene 5, Juliet: _____

_____

_____

_____

Prereading

Name _____ Date _____

> A. Look ahead at the art in Act 2. Think about what might happen in this act. Read the choices below. Put a check mark by the one that seems most likely. Then give a reason why you think so.

---

1. Scene 2, art on page 25.

What do you think is happening in this picture?

_____ Romeo is saying it is too dangerous for them to see each other.

_____ Romeo got lost in the garden and is asking Juliet how he can get out.

_____ Romeo and Juliet are declaring their love for each other.

_____ Juliet is saying that Romeo better go away or she will call her father.

Explain why you think this is the most likely choice. _____

_____

2. Scene 6, art on page 38.

What do you think is happening in this picture?

_____ Romeo and Juliet will soon be married by the Friar.

_____ The Friar will tell them to stop seeing each other.

_____ The Friar will soon tell Juliet's father to keep an eye on his daughter.

_____ Romeo and Juliet want the Friar to give them Latin lessons.

Explain why you think this is the most likely choice. _____

_____

_____

> B. Look again at the picture on page 25. What do you think is going through each character's mind? Write your answer on the lines below.

_____

_____

_____

Character Study

Name _____ Date _____

Read the following lines from Act 2. Put a check mark by the group of words that best completes the statement. Then answer the question that follows.

---

1. Mercutio laughs at love's scars, / But he never felt a wound. (page 23)

   Romeo means that Mercutio:

   _____ wins every fight he is in

   _____ has never been in love

   _____ does not have a good sense of humor

   _____ has a good sense of humor

   What are two words that could describe Mercutio? _____

2. What's in a name? / A rose by any other name/Would smell as sweet. (page 24)

   Juliet means that:

   _____ Romeo's last name should be Rose instead of Montague

   _____ roses are no better than any other flowers

   _____ if Romeo's name were Tim, he would still be wonderful

   _____ roses should be called tulips

   How might Juliet have completed the following lines?

   The moon by any other name would _____ .

   A pizza by any other name would _____ .

   A puppy by any other name would _____ .

3. There's a count by the name of Paris. / He wants to marry Juliet himself. / She would rather kiss a toad than look at him. (page 34)

   By these words, we know that Juliet:

   _____ likes to kiss toads

   _____ does not like Paris

   _____ thinks Paris looks like a toad

   _____ wants to marry Paris

   What else does this show about Juliet? _____

Key Words

Name _____ Date _____

A. Read each of the following sentences taken from the play. Use context clues or a dictionary to figure out the meaning of the word or phrase in dark type. If you need more clues, find the sentence in the play. Fill in the box next to the best definition. Then answer the question that follows.

---

1. Their brightness would **confuse** the birds. (page 23)

   ☐ blind   ☐ mix up   ☐ scare   ☐ amaze

   Write about a time you were confused about something.

   _____

   _____

2. **Deny** your father and change your name. (page 24)

   ☐ surprise   ☐ love   ☐ leave   ☐ reject

   Tell about a time you denied something.

   _____

   _____

3. What dies is born again in great **variety**. (page 29)

   ☐ colors   ☐ beauty   ☐ many kinds☐ numbers

   What do you think a "variety store" is?

   _____

   _____

4. Are you really so **eager**? (page 36)

   ☐ enthusiastic   ☐ bored   ☐ unhappy   ☐ brave

   Describe the last time you were eager to do something.

   _____

   _____

B. Now choose one of the sentences or groups of sentences in Part A. Use it as the beginning of a story. Write some more sentences to go with that story beginning. Try to use some of the other words in dark type. Start your story on the back of this sheet.

Point of View   **4**

Name _____   Date _____

The point of view in this play changes from scene to scene, depending on
which character or characters are on stage. Think about each of the
following scenes. Rewrite each one from the point of view suggested.
Reread the pages in parentheses if necessary. Use the back of this sheet if
you need more room to write.

---

1. Most of Act 2, Scene 1 is from the point of view of Benvolio and Mercutio.
   How might it have been different if told from Romeo's point of view ? Write a
   speech that Romeo might have made, as he listened to Benvolio and
   Mercutio calling him. (pages 22–23)

   _____

   _____

   _____

   _____

   _____

2. Toward the end of Act 2, Scene 2, the Nurse calls Juliet to come inside. If the
   audience could see the Nurse, what would she be doing and saying? Write a
   short speech the Nurse might have made at this time. Add some stage
   directions that tell what she might be doing. (page 28)

   _____

   _____

   _____

   _____

   _____

3. The audience does not see the wedding ceremony performed by Friar
   Laurence. Write that scene, adding an aside from Friar Laurence. If you don't
   know what an "aside" is, see your Glossary for a definition. (page 37–39)

   _____

   _____

   _____

   _____

   _____

Language Lab

Name _____   Date _____

A **simile** is a figure of speech that compares two unlike things, using the
word *like* or *as*. A **metaphor** is a figure of speech that compares two
unlike things, without the use of *like* or *as*. Read each of the following
examples from the play. Write *simile* or *metaphor* to tell what it is. Then
write another simile or metaphor that expresses the same idea. The first
one has been done as an example.

---

1. It is the east and Juliet is the sun! (page 23)

   This is an example of a <u>metaphor</u>.

   Your own example: <u>It is the frame and Juliet is the picture!</u>

2. It's too much like the lightning, which is gone / Before you know it. (page 27)

   This is an example of a _____.

   Your own example: _____

3. This bud of our love, so tender and so sweet, / May grow to a flower when
   next we meet. (page 27)

   This is an example of a _____.

   Your own example: _____

4. If I just mention him, / She turns as white as a sheet. (page 34)

   This is an example of a _____.

   Your own example: _____

5. If she were young and in love, / She would move as quickly as a rolling ball.
   (page 34)

   This is an example of a _____.

   Your own example: _____

6. They are like fire and gunpowder— / When they meet, they destroy each
   other. (page 37)

   This is an example of a _____.

   Your own example: _____

Reading for the Main Idea

Name _____   Date _____

> Look back at Act 2. Put a check mark by the title that best describes each scene. Then write a title of your own for each scene.

1. A good title for Scene 1 would be:

    _____ Mercutio Casts a Magic Spell

    _____ Romeo Hides

    Your own title: _____

2. A good title for Scene 2 would be:

    _____ Romeo Lingers in the Garden

    _____ Romeo and Juliet Declare Their Love

    Your own title: _____

3. A good title for Scene 3 would be:

    _____ The Friar Agrees to the Marriage

    _____ The Friar Scolds Romeo

    Your own title: _____

4. A good title for Scene 4 would be:

    _____ Romeo Tells the Nurse the Plan

    _____ The Nurse Looks for Romeo

    Your own title: _____

5. A good title for Scene 5 would be:

    _____ The Nurse Is Out of Breath

    _____ The Nurse Tells Juliet the Plan

    Your own title: _____

6. A good title for Scene 6 would be:

    _____ Romeo and Juliet Meet for Their Wedding

    _____ The Joys in Life

    Your own title: _____

Challenge

Name _____   Date _____

Scene 2 is often called "the balcony scene". In this romantic scene, Romeo and Juliet declare their love and make plans to marry. We already know, from the Prologue, that this will lead to their deaths. Imagine that Juliet recognizes how dangerous their love affair is. She has decided to listen to her head instead of her heart. She decides to reject Romeo and avoid any tragedy. Rewrite the balcony scene to show how Juliet does this. If you need more room to write, use the back of this sheet.

_____
_____
_____
_____
_____
_____
_____
_____
_____
_____
_____
_____
_____
_____
_____
_____

Prereading

Name _____ Date _____

A. The lines below appear in Act 3. Read them and put a check in front of what you think will happen next. Base your prediction on what you already know about the characters. Then write answers to the questions that follow.

---

1. Benvolio: Good Mercutio, let's go home. / The day is hot, and the Capulets out. / If we meet, we will probably get into a fight.

   _____ Mercutio will agree with Benvolio, and they will go home.

   _____ Mercutio will tell Benvolio that he's not afraid of a fight.

   _____ Mercutio will tell Benvolio that the day will soon get cooler.

   _____ Mercutio will refuse to go home, so Benvolio will force him.

   Why do you think this is the most likely choice?

   _____

2. Capulet: I tell you this, Juliet: Marry Paris, / Or leave this house. Beg! Starve! / Die in the streets! I will cut you out of my will!

   _____ Juliet's father will change his mind as soon as Juliet cries.

   _____ Juliet will leave her father's house and live in the streets as a beggar.

   _____ Juliet will do as her father asks and marry Paris.

   _____ Juliet will continue to refuse to marry Paris.

   Why do you think this is the most likely choice?

   _____

B. Look at the art on page 49. What do you think is happening? On the lines below, write a paragraph telling what you think. Save this paper. When you finish reading Act 3, compare your answer to the play. Were you right?

_____

_____

_____

Exercise

2

Character Study

Name _____ Date _____

A. Each sentence below describes a character in the play. Read each
   one. On the line, write the name of the person who is being described.
   Use these names: Romeo, Juliet, Benvolio, Mercutio, Tybalt, Capulet,
   Lady Capulet, the Nurse, Prince Escalus, and Friar Laurence.

---

1. This character defends Romeo in a sword fight with a Capulet.

_____

2. Romeo fights this character with a sword and kills him.

_____

3. This character gives Juliet a drink that will make her appear dead.

_____

4. This character must leave Verona.

_____

5. This character brings terrible news to Juliet.

_____

6. This character is the ruler of Verona.

_____

7. This character tells Juliet to stop crying over her cousin's death.

_____

8. This character once quarreled about old laces in new shoes.

_____

9. This character's cousin was killed in a duel.

_____

10. This character decides that Juliet will be married in a few days.

_____

B. Choose one of the characters described above. On the back of this
   sheet, write a more complete description of the person. Describe the
   person physically. Then tell something about the character's
   personality.

Key Words

Name _____ Date _____

> A. Read the definitions. Then complete the sentences by writing the correct word in each blank.

1. **quarrel**   to argue, to disagree

    slash   a sweeping stroke or cut

    excuse   a reason given to explain or justify something

    insult   to treat in a rude and inconsiderate way

    Tybalt was looking for Romeo in order to _____ him. He was hoping for an _____ to start a fight. Tybalt was very skilled with his sword, and one _____ could really do some harm. The slightest reason for a _____ might start a big fight.

2. **jealous**   full of envy

    weeping   crying, shedding tears

    farewell good-bye

    comfort   to make someone feel better in time of grief

    Romeo tried to _____ Juliet in their time of sorrow. After spending just one night as a married couple, they had to say _____. As Juliet was_____, they were both hoping they could be together again soon. If Paris had seen how much they were in love, he would probably have been _____.

> B. After you read Act 3, look through it again. Pick out four words that you think your classmates might not know. In your own words, write a definition for each one. Then use each word in a sentence that would help your classmates better understand it.

1. _____

    _____

2. _____

    _____

3. _____

    _____

4. _____

    _____

Point of View

Name _____ Date _____

> Put yourself in the place of each of the following characters. What are you thinking during each of the following scenes? Write your thoughts on the lines below.

1. You are Romeo. You have just come from your wedding at Friar Laurence's cell. You run into Tybalt, now your new relative. Tybalt starts to insult you.

   _____

   _____

   _____

   _____

2. You are Romeo. Your friend Mercutio has just been killed. His last words to you were to blame you for getting in the way.

   _____

   _____

   _____

   _____

3. You are Juliet, and you have just found out the terrible news. Your cousin has been killed by your new husband.

   _____

   _____

   _____

   _____

4. You are Juliet's father. You don't know anything about Juliet's love for Romeo. Juliet has just told you that she does not want to marry Paris.

   _____

   _____

   _____

Language Lab

Name _____ Date _____

> The lines below come from the play. Read them, and answer the questions that follow.

1. You once quarreled with a man for coughing / Because he woke up your dog. (page 41)

   Think about a time you had a silly argument with someone. Describe the situation, telling why you quarreled and what happened next.

   _____

   _____

2. I am like a child the night before a party, / Who cannot yet wear the new party clothes. (pages 45-46)

   Tell about a time you really looked forward to something that you knew would happen soon.

   _____

   _____

3. Oh, the heart of a serpent! / Devil looking like an angel! Evil posing as good! / Oh, that such evil could live in such beauty! (page 46)

   Were you ever surprised that someone who seemed good was not really good? Describe what happened and how you felt about it. You may wish to write about someone you know, someone in the news, or a character in a movie.

   _____

   _____

4. There is no world but Verona for me. / My whole life is here. (page 49)

   Do you feel this way about the place in which you live? Why or why not?

   _____

   _____

5. The lighter it gets, / The darker are our problems. (page 54)

   Tell about a time it seemed that your own problems or those of a friend were getting worse.

   _____

   _____

Giving Advice

Name _____ Date _____

A. Imagine that you are Juliet's best friend. You can see that she is torn between wanting to please her parents and keeping her vows to Romeo. You want to help her. What advice would you give her?. Read the suggestions below. Write your own suggestion for number 4. Draw a star next to the best suggestion.

---

1. Tell your father the truth—that you can't marry Paris because you are already married. Maybe your father can help get a pardon for Romeo, and you can soon be reunited.

2. Tell Paris the truth, and ask him to tell your father that he has changed his mind.

3. Run away from Verona and go to Mantua to be with Romeo.

4. Your own suggestion: _____

_____

_____

B. Now write what you would say to Juliet. Be sure to give some good reasons for following your advice. You might wish to warn Juliet about what her life will be like if she does not follow your advice. Begin your advice on the lines below. Use the back of this sheet if you need more room.

_____

_____

_____

_____

_____

_____

_____

Challenge

Name _____ Date _____

A. In Romeo and Juliet's time, it was not unusual for parents to arrange their children's marriages. Such marriages were based on wealth, social position, and property. Romance was not considered very important. In fact, romantic love as a good reason for marriage is a fairly modern idea.

Imagine that Romeo, like Paris, had come to Juliet's father to ask for her hand. Put yourself in Lord Capulet's place. Fill out the following lists, from his point of view.

Juliet Marries Paris

Reasons For   Reasons Against

_____   _____

_____   _____

_____   _____

Juliet Marries Romeo

Reasons For   Reasons Against

_____   _____

_____   _____

_____   _____

B. Now put yourself in Juliet's place. Fill out the same lists, from your point of view.

I Marry Paris

Reasons For   Reasons Against

_____   _____

_____   _____

_____   _____

I Marry Romeo

Reasons For   Reasons Against

_____   _____

_____   _____

_____   _____

Prereading

Name _____ Date _____

> A. Look at the art in Acts 4 and 5. Then answer the questions below.

1. In Act 4, what do you think is happening in the picture on page 61?

   _____

   _____

   What makes you think so?

   _____

   _____

2. In Act 4, what do you think is happening in the picture on page 65?

   _____

   _____

   What makes you think so?

   _____

   _____

3. In Act 5, what do you think is happening in the picture on page 77?

   _____

   _____

   What makes you think so?

   _____

   _____

4. In Act 5, what do you think is happening in the picture on page 84?

   _____

   _____

   What makes you think so?

   _____

   _____

> B. Save this paper. When you finish reading the book, compare your
> answers to what actually happened.

Character Study

Name _____   Date _____

A. Imagine that you are a lawyer. The following people have been accused of wrongdoing in the deaths of Romeo and Juliet: Friar Laurence, the Nurse, and the Druggist in Mantua. You are trying to decide which of the three has a better chance of winning the case. So you interview each one to see what they can say to defend their actions. What do you think each one would say? Write your answers on the lines.

---

1. FRIAR LAURENCE: I did nothing wrong in this case. The reasons I say so are

_____

_____

_____

2. NURSE: I did nothing wrong in this case. The reasons I say so are

_____

_____

_____

3. DRUGGIST IN MANTUA: I did nothing wrong in this case. The reasons I say so are

_____

_____

_____

B. After your interviews, you have chosen which of the three you will represent. Write your choice here: _____
On the lines below, write the speech you will make to the judge. This speech will sum up your arguments in defense of your client. Use the back of this sheet if you need more room.

_____

_____

Key Words

Name _____ Date _____

> Read these sentences from the play. Put a check by the meaning used in the play. Then write a sentence using the word in its other meaning.

1. PARIS: It was Lord Capulet's idea. / It is fine with me. (page 59)

   _____ **fine**   very well; all right

   _____ **fine**   a sum of money to be paid for breaking a law or rule

   Sentence using other meaning: _____
   _____

2. JULIET: Dear Nurse, please leave me alone / For the rest of the night. (page 64)

   _____ **rest**   to be still or quiet

   _____ **rest**   remainder; what is left

   Sentence using other meaning: _____
   _____

3. ROMEO: Last night, I dreamed that Juliet / Found me lying dead . . . (page 73)

   _____ **lying**   being in a flat, horizontal position

   _____ **lying**   saying something not true in order to deceive

   Sentence using other meaning: _____
   _____

4. FRIAR LAURENCE: Bring it to my cell right away. (page 76)

   _____ **cell**   the tiny, basic unit of all matter

   _____ **cell**   a small room, as for a prisoner or a monk

   Sentence using other meaning: _____
   _____

5. JULIET: Did you drink it all and leave no friendly drop / To help me follow you? (page 81)

   _____ **drop**   to fall suddenly

   _____ **drop**   a small amount of liquid in a somewhat round shape

   Sentence using other meaning: _____
   _____

Point of View

Name _____ Date _____

A. Put yourself in Paris's place. Remember that he has followed the customs of the day and has done nothing wrong. Read his lines in Act 4, Scene 1. This is the first and only time Paris and Juliet are seen together. Write a diary entry he might have written after seeing her.

_____

_____

_____

_____

_____

B. Now read Paris's lines in Act 4, Scene 5, when he finds out that Juliet is dead. Also read his lines in Act 5, Scene 3, when he meets Romeo for the first time. Notice that the first thing Paris wants to do is arrest Romeo, not fight with him. If you were giving the speech at Paris's funeral, what would you say about him?

_____

_____

_____

_____

_____

_____

_____

_____

_____

Language Lab

Name _____ Date _____

A. What do you think each of the following lines means? Fill in the box next to the best answer. Then write another answer that could also be true.

---

1. She cries so much over Tybalt's death / That I have not had a chance to court her. (page 59)

   _____ Paris has not had a chance to play tennis with Juliet.

   _____ Paris has not had a chance to speak to Juliet about love.

   _____ Paris has not yet filed legal papers about their marriage.

   Another good answer: _____

2. Death, that has taken her / To make me cry, / Ties up my tongue and will not let me speak. (page 69)

   _____ Capulet's tongue is in a knot.

   _____ Capulet is so upset he can't even talk.

   _____ Capulet thinks Death is a real person.

   Another good answer: _____

3. I will put these flowers on your bridal bed. / I will water them with my tears every night. (page 76)

   _____ Paris is saying he will cry for Juliet for a long time.

   _____ Paris will actually cry over the flowers to water them.

   _____ Paris thinks tears are better than regular water for flowers.

   Another good answer: _____

4. PARIS: You are as good as dead!

   ROMEO: That is true, and that is why I am here. (page 78)

   _____ Romeo is dying of a rare disease.

   _____ Romeo is saying he can't live without Juliet and will soon be dead.

   _____ Romeo thinks death is better than life.

   Another good answer: _____

B. Choose one of the lines in Part A. Think of a time when the idea in that sentence might have applied to you, someone you know, or a character in a movie. Describe the situation on the back of this sheet.

Writing a News Story

Name _____   Date _____

> A. Imagine that you are a reporter for a daily newspaper. You are writing
>   a story explaining to the townspeople why Juliet had two funerals.
>   Explain all the facts and evidence in the story. Be sure to include
>   information that answers the questions *who, what, when, where,* and
>   *why.* Write your news report on the lines below. Include a headline.

_____

_____

_____

_____

_____

_____

_____

_____

_____

_____

_____

> B. Find an interesting article in a current newspaper. How is each of the
>   following questions answered in the article?

Who? _____

What? _____

When? _____

Where? _____

Why? _____

Challenge

Name _____ Date _____

Pretend that you are either Romeo or Juliet, and you survived that night at the Capulet tomb. It is 10 years later. Write a short essay about your life over the last 10 years. Explain how you managed to survive. Tell what you've been doing since then.

You may wish to consider these questions: Did both of you survive? Was any punishment necessary for the death of Paris? Did you have children? Did you continue to live in Verona? How did your relationship with your parents work out after that? Was there a big wedding and/or reception? Did the family feud continue? What happened to Friar Laurence? Was the Druggist in Verona punished?

Final Exam, page 1

Name _____   Date _____

A. Fill in the box next to the best answer.

---

1. What were the names of the families who were feuding when the play opened?

   ☐ Verona and Mantua   ☐ Romeo and Paris
   ☐ Laurence and Paris   ☐ Montague and Capulet

2. Where did most of the action of the play take place?

   ☐ Verona, Italy   ☐ Mantua, Italy
   ☐ London, England   ☐ An unnamed town

3. Why was Romeo so sad when the play opened?

   ☐ He loved Juliet, but she didn't love him.
   ☐ He loved Rosaline, but she didn't love him.
   ☐ His parents wouldn't let him play music.
   ☐ He did not know how to fence very well.

4. Why did Romeo agree to go to the party at the Capulet home?

   ☐ Rosaline would be there.   ☐ Juliet would be there.
   ☐ He had nothing else to do. ☐ He wanted to make trouble for the Capulets.

5. Whom did Lord Capulet want Juliet to talk to at the party?

   ☐ Rosaline   ☐ Tybalt
   ☐ Romeo   ☐ Paris

6. When did Romeo and Juliet declare their love for each other?

   ☐ three days after they met ☐ the same night they met
   ☐ the moment they met   ☐ never

7. Why did Romeo have to leave Verona?

   ☐ Juliet's father found out about them.   ☐ He had a new job.
   ☐ He killed Tybalt in a duel.   ☐ He killed Mercutio in a duel.

8. What was the topic of Friar Laurence's message to Romeo?

   ☐ news in Verona   ☐ a possible job in Mantua
   ☐ a pardon from Prince Escalus   ☐ the plan concerning Juliet

9. What caused Romeo's death?

   ☐ He was stabbed during a duel with Paris.
   ☐ He took poison.
   ☐ He stabbed himself with his dagger.
   ☐ He died of grief over Juliet.

10. What happened to Romeo's mother?

   ☐ She died of grief after Romeo was sent away.
   ☐ She went out of her mind.
   ☐ She moved away.
   ☐ She decided never to leave the house again.

Final Exam, page 2

Name _____ Date _____

> B. Write two sentences about each of the following characters. In the first
> one, tell about a quality in that character's personality. In the
> second one, tell something that character does.

---

1. Romeo: _____
   _____
   _____
   _____

2. Juliet: _____
   _____
   _____
   _____

3. Mercutio: _____
   _____
   _____
   _____

4. Paris: _____
   _____
   _____
   _____

5. Nurse: _____
   _____
   _____
   _____

6. Friar Laurence: _____
   _____
   _____
   _____

7. Lord Capulet: _____
   _____
   _____
   _____

8. Prince Escalus: _____
   _____

Choose Your Own Project

Name _____ Date _____

Choose one project from each section.

Alone:

- Based on Mercutio's description of Queen Mab, draw a picture of her as she goes about her nightly activities. Look back at Act 1, Scene 4 to refresh your memory.

- Create a valentine that Romeo might have designed to send to Rosaline. Then create a valentine that he might have designed to send to Juliet from Mantua. Try to show how Romeo's idea of love had changed after he met Juliet.

- Write one of the following letters:

    a. The letter Friar Laurence wrote to Romeo, which was never delivered to him in Mantua. This was the letter that explained the plan.

    b. The letter Romeo wrote and gave to Balthasar. This was the letter addressed to Romeo's father, which Prince Escalus read to himself in the last scene.

    c. A letter Romeo might have written to Prince Escalus, asking for pardon and explaining the circumstances.

With a partner:

- Using clay or papier-mâché, make models of the statues that Lord Capulet and Lord Montague planned to build to honor their children.

- Design and produce a poster to advertise a new movie version of the play. You may wish to look at some movie posters to get ideas about what should go on yours. Think about which actors would be good in the roles, and include their names in your poster. Put your poster on display in the classroom.

With a group:

- Act out your favorite scene from the play. Be sure that each person in your group contributes to this project. One or more persons can make or obtain necessary props. Others can take the roles of the actors. Other jobs include that of director and sound-effects person. Rehearse until you feel comfortable with the scene, and then present it to the class.

- Make up a new scene that would have changed the outcome of the play. For example, what if Juliet had told her parents that she was married to Romeo? Or what if Romeo had told his friends? Or what if the Druggist had refused to sell the poison to Romeo? Act out your scene for the class.

Working with the Glossary

Name _____ Date _____

Before completing this page, you may wish to look once more at the glossary your teacher has given you. Review the definitions of any of the terms used below.

Comparisons Find two comparisons the author makes to give you a dramatic picture of a character, scene, or event.

_____

_____

_____

_____

Conflict Find at least one example of a conflict between two characters or between a character and an event. Then find one example of a conflict *within* a character.

_____

_____

_____

_____

Dialogue Find at least two lines of dialogue that best express the hopes of two of the major characters in the story.

Character 1: _____

_____

_____

Character 2: _____

_____

_____

Point of View From whose point of view was this story told? (Which character?)

_____

Choose another major character in the story. Then describe how the story might have been different if it had been told from this character's point of view. Use the back of this sheet.

Sequencing the Story

Name _____   Date _____

List six events from the book in the sequence in which they occurred. Then cut out the six boxes below and exchange them with a classmate. Now take your classmate's work and arrange those boxes in the correct sequence of events. When you're done, check each other's work.

```
┌─────────────────────────────────────────────────┐
│                                                 │
│                                                 │
│                                                 │
└─────────────────────────────────────────────────┘
                          ↓
┌─────────────────────────────────────────────────┐
│                                                 │
│                                                 │
│                                                 │
└─────────────────────────────────────────────────┘
                          ↓
┌─────────────────────────────────────────────────┐
│                                                 │
│                                                 │
│                                                 │
└─────────────────────────────────────────────────┘
                          ↓
┌─────────────────────────────────────────────────┐
│                                                 │
│                                                 │
│                                                 │
└─────────────────────────────────────────────────┘
                          ↓
┌─────────────────────────────────────────────────┐
│                                                 │
│                                                 │
│                                                 │
└─────────────────────────────────────────────────┘
                          ↓
┌─────────────────────────────────────────────────┐
│                                                 │
│                                                 │
│                                                 │
└─────────────────────────────────────────────────┘
```

Understanding the Times, page 1

Name _____ Date _____

Time and place shape our lives. People who lived 200 years ago faced different circumstances than we do now. They did different work, listened to different music, and had a different view of the world. And people who live in busy crowded places have always looked at life differently than people who live in far-off country corners.

Story characters also exist in a framework of time and place. Where and when the story unfolds often determine the events the characters must deal with. This exercise will deepen your understanding of how the events of the story were influenced by the time and place. In order to complete the exercise, you may need to do research outside the classroom.

PART A GEOGRAPHY/HISTORY

1. About how many years ago does the story take place? _____

2. In what century does the story take place? _____

    In what year or years? _____

3. Was this a time of peace or war? Of plenty or want? Of freedom or lack of freedom? Write three sentences to describe the mood of the time.

    _____

    _____

    _____

4. In what country does the story take place? _____

    In what city or region? _____

    Was this a real city or a fictional one? _____

5. Who was the leader of the country at this time?_____

    _____

PART B THE ARTS

1. Name three famous artists from the era (time period) in which the story

    takes place. _____

    _____   _____

2. Name one famous painting by each artist named above.

    _____   _____

    _____

Name _____ Date _____

3. What type of music were people listening to at the time of the story?

   _____

4. Name two famous composers or musicians from the era of the story.

   _____   _____

5. Name one famous musical piece for each person named above.

   _____   _____

PART C   DAILY LIFE

Take two of the major characters from the story and answer the questions below.

1. What kinds of work did these characters do?

   _____   _____

2. Do people today do the same kinds of work?

   _____

3. Choose one of the two characters from above. Write a paragraph explaining how his or her job has changed from what it was back then to what it is today. Write on the back of this sheet or on another sheet of paper.

4. Write a paragraph describing each item below. Write on the back of this sheet or on another sheet of paper.
   (a) a typical day of work for the character chosen above;
   (b) a typical day of work for a person today who has the same job;
   (c) a typical evening at home for the character chosen above;
   (d) a typical evening at home for someone today who has a similar lifestyle
      to the character above.